Bad Tax Idea,
Good Tax Idea

By

Kim Isaac Greenblatt

Published By Kim Greenblatt
Los Angeles, California, USA

2

Bad Tax Idea, Good Tax Idea
by Kim Isaac Greenblatt

Published by Kim Greenblatt   in Los Angeles, California, USA.
ISBN-10 0-9777282-6-9
ISBN-13 978-0-9777282-6-8

August 2007

Dedicated to Colonel Burton Ross McKee, retired and "The Master" of taxes, Craig Thomas, E.A.

I am always learning from both of them!

4

Contents

6

INTRODUCTION

I've been preparing tax returns for several years and I've found that there are a lot of bad ideas and misconceptions about tax preparation as well as a lot of good ideas. The purpose of this book is to get you thinking about your own tax situation and get you some information that might end up saving you hundreds or thousands or even hundreds of thousands of dollars legally at tax time.

There are some horrible misconceptions out in the marketplace as well as unscrupulous people who promise you the lowest possible taxes. A lot of that is rubbish. You are the one that is making the money, you are the one responsible for paying the taxes. No matter what people promise you, it is your signature on the tax return that is saying that to the best of your knowledge the information you are providing is true. Isn't it easier to understand your own tax situation and then consult an honest professional to help you with your options? Well, I hope it is easier for you to do that! When I have clients come in and are worried about taking a legitimate deduction (notice how I said LEGITIMATE DEDUCTION) "If you have the receipts to back up your deductions, you should have no problems."

You should feel that way as well! As hard as it is to believe, the Internal Revenue Service (IRS) and the state tax authorities don't have any problems with you taking legitimate deductions. If you can support your claim, then there is nothing to worry about. If you are trying to pull a scam, that is another issue, you are opening up a hornet's nest and I don't want to do your tax return!

Tax planning is not that complicated – it just requires, well, some planning and some time to understand the current tax laws.

Now we may have some issues because some current tax laws are about as easy to understand as nuclear physics or graduate

level calculus Some are VERY complicated
and you need to consult a professional or at
the very least re-read the tax rules to
understand some of them. If you don't
believe me, try figuring depreciation
between Federal taxes and state taxes (such
as California) where California did not do
any special adjustments for depreciation!

The book is in response to some clients (or
even some tax professionals) who want
some ideas for their own situations. I
figured, if they wanted some ideas, there
are dozens of people who want some
information and didn't think to ask the
questions themselves but will appreciate
the answers once they see it.
If nothing else, you might learn one or two
things and that alone is worth the cost of
the book in saving or making you some
money.

Kim Greenblatt
July 21, 2007
West Hills, California

10

Bad Tax Idea: Getting married without checking on the tax ramifications. A lot of couples hear that "getting married is great for tax purposes". It can be but, if you do it wrong (and a lot of couples goof it up their first year) you both may end up owing money.

You are considered married for tax purposes on the last day of the year.

Here is an all-to-common scenario that happens:

John makes $72,000 as an Engineer and for filing single for 2007 with one exemption would have a tax liability (ballpark) of $13,424. This takes into account his standard deduction and status.

Suzy makes $30,000 as a Teacher and for filing single for 2007 with one exemption would have a tax liability (ballpark) of $3509. This takes into account his standard deduction and status.

If they decide to get married and have not started to take into account their tax liability they potentially can face:

Joint income: $102,000 and a ballpark estimate of their tax liability then is $15848 which is lower than $13424 + 3509 or $16,933.

But the problem is that both John and Suzy, anticipating that they would be married each changed their Form W-4 at work to indicate Married Filing Jointly and they each took two allowances. Let's say for this example that they only had $10,848 withheld. It turns out they did NOT have enough money deducted to pay for their taxes! They end up with sticker shock at tax season the following year and can't understand why they owe $5000.

Maybe they didn't change anything but their Human Resources Dept did not update their tax tables and they did not withhold enough taxes. It happens. In any event, the tax burden would be on our heroes, John and Suzy..

Good Tax Idea: When you start planning for your wedding (or if you are going to elope) and you work for somebody - go to your human resources department and change your W-4 only after you have sat down and crunched the numbers as to what your combined income will be. Once you know your tax bracket, and depending on what you want as a couple - Do you both want a refund? Do you both want to owe just a little? Plan your deductions accordingly.

If you both are in doubt, keep your filing status as Single, with zero deductions for the first year or just one each. If it looks like you are going to owe more money you can have your Human Resources department withhold an extra amount of money each paycheck to cover the tax shortfall.

If you both work as independent contractors (that means you receive a 1099 form) and are filing quarterly taxes (for Fed and for state depending on what state you live in) make sure that you are socking away enough money to cover the quarterly payments.

A very general rule of thumb is that the person in the marriage who makes the most money should take the exemptions on his or her W-4. The other person should generally take a single filing status with zero or one allowances.

The form I suggest you reference from the IRS is: Publication 919: How do I Adjust My Tax Withholding? For your respective state I suggest you visit one of the sites listed at the end of the book or check with a web search engine.

Bad Tax Idea: Bad recordkeeping.

How many times has it been tax time and you were putting your paperwork together and realized that you forgot something? Or even worse, that you lost your receipts that you had paid cash for. This will makes difficult at tax time when you are trying to piece together what you can take as a deduction or as an expense.

Good Tax Idea: Get an expanding folder or large plastic container with a lid and start to collect in envelopes your receipts. Label each envelope with its respective category - medical, business, expenses, children's college, rental property, quarterly taxes paid etc. Once a month, take totals for everything you have for that month and keep a running total on an electronic spreadsheet or word processing document of your choice.

If you have a business you should know
better and have accurate and detailed
books. Running software isn't going to help
you if you don't take the time to enter the
data into the system and periodically take a
pulse as to how the business is running.

Set up one date where you can take
inventory and see if you have all the bank
statements, credit card receipts, customer
invoices, etc that you need to help
determine accurately what state your
finances are in and what your tax situation
is.

If it looks like you are earning more money
than you thought, congratulations. Make
sure you are putting enough aside to cover
quarterly taxes or have additional taxes
withheld from your "day W-2" job.

If it looks like you might be paying too
much, adjust the payments down but be
careful that you don't accidentally go the
other way and end up not having enough
withheld or paid for that quarter!

The other part of this is please make sure that at tax time you have SUMMARIES of the different categories that are using and don't resort to having to dig into your folders (or, gasp, shoebox) to get receipts. Whether you do your own taxes on the web or with software or go to a professional, you want to save time and aggravation by having everything accessible.

You'll thank me for this later...

Bad Tax Idea: No receipts or cash only for charitable contributions.

Good Idea: Effective 2007, actually late in 2006 if one wants to be exact; the IRS decreed that in order to claim contributions for charity.

If you make weekly contributions to your church, synagogue or mosque, please make sure that you do it by check instead of coins in the collection plates. The IRS wants to see a track record of the donations - and you should too. Don't be afraid to donate non-cash items - just make sure that you get them appraised and insure that you get a letter from the charity saying what purpose they are using the items for. The appraiser, by the way, needs to be an expert in his or her field and can't arbitrarily say that the old bag of shoes you donated were worth $1000, unless of course, you had $2000 of gold inlay in the heels of the soles....

Bad Tax Idea: Not thinking about what happens when you cash out of an IRA or 401K early or fail to roll them over properly.

You may have been laid off and as one of the terms of employment; your employer sends you a letter and or the check from your 401K. Maybe you have been on hard times and need your money and you cash out your IRA. You will need to put aside at least a third of it for paying Fed and state taxes.

Take care of this immediately because more times than not, if you are financially strapped for cash, you may be in a worse situation several months down the line at tax time and you may have more penalties incurred for not having enough money withheld or paid quarterly.

Good Tax Idea: Putting aside and paying at least a third of your disbursement quarterly to the IRS and state taxing agencies to cover any tax liability incurred by cashing out your IRA or 401K.

Bad Tax Idea: Filing an amended return before your original return has hit the IRS or the state taxing agency.

With the prevalence of software and websites that let you file for yourself, you are inclined to jump right in and e-file to get back any refund that you are anticipating. Then boom, without fail, - a W-2 comes from a part time job you forgot about or you get a Form t 1099-INT for a savings account that you forgot about as well.

Looks like you had an extra $500 in income that there wasn't enough tax taken out for or you earned interest for $123.

Ugh.

So you decide to amend your tax return.

The correct thing to do is first wait until you get back your refund from the Fed (and state if you filed and are expecting a refund there as well). The IRS and state taxing agency may correct it for you. They may not. It is only after you have received your refund that you should file and then prepare the amended tax return and pay back whatever it is that you might owe. Who knows, maybe you will find something else you missed and you might get a larger refund.

The reason you need to wait before filing an amended return is that the amended returns are processed at different departments than the regular tax returns. Sometimes it takes months for them to get processed. There IS a chance; however, that the amended return might get processed before the first return you filed and you don't want that to happen! If things get filed backwards, the IRS and/or

state tax authority will be sending you a
letter!

**Good Tax Idea: Try to exercise some
patience and wait till you get all your tax
forms from your banks and employers.
If in doubt, call them or check on their
websites to see when they are sending
out their forms. Verify that they are the
final forms!**

Sometimes banks send out corrected 1099-
INTS and if that is the case, you need to
amend your tax return accordingly..

Bad Tax Idea: Throwing away last year's
tax return.

Please hold onto your tax returns for at
least three years, longer if you have
investment property or real estate that you
will need to research to calculate basis.
You will also need the prior year's tax
return if you are filing electronically and
need to get your prior year's adjusted gross

income or information for basis, carry-forward of losses, etc. Find somewhere and keep a hardcopy of it safe - as well as an electronic copy if you can.

Good Tax Idea: Have one central spot or filing cabinet where you store all your tax information. You will be able to refer to it all year and store receipts and other documentation there as well. This will be very helpful if you are applying for a home or business loan!

Bad Tax Idea: Not running the numbers or having your tax preparer run the numbers to see if it is better to itemize or take the standard deduction.

Good Tax Idea: Take the time and either run the numbers yourself or have your tax preparer do it for you.

One of the most common scenarios for me each year is people assuming that they do not have enough deductions to itemize. It is important that you either take the time to run the deductions yourself or have a competent tax preparer to ask you the digging questions (and some of the software out on the market might be good enough if you actually learn to use it otherwise see a professional!).

Common places where you might exceed the standard deductions - you had a bad year for medical expenses and paid lots and lots of money out of pocket for doctor visits, x-rays, prescriptions, medical premiums - you get the idea.

Another example is running scenario changes where a child is included in a parent's return and where he isn't. It is a good idea to run the numbers and suggest that the parents work out with their child what an equitable disbursal of funds would be if the child cannot claim himself (in the example of a child actor or a child attending college). Sometimes divorced parents who are still in a cordial relationship work the numbers and come to an agreement between themselves that way when it comes to splitting custody. It is a good idea to plan for that though in the prior year to meet residency and/or support requirements...

Bad Tax Idea: Generally Married Filing Separately is a bad tax idea. Unless you have specific reasons for it, don't do it.

This happens to me every year. Couples come in and ask me if it is better to file Married Filing Jointly or Married Filing Separately. Generally, it is always better to go with MFJ but in some cases there may be reasons that as a couple it would benefit them to file separately. I always take the time to run the numbers both ways to see which way is better for my clients. You should too!

Bad Tax Idea: Not Amending Tax Returns if you have to.

If you discover income that was received and you didn't include it, don't panic. Just file an amended tax return. You have up to three years to get it in but bear in mind that if the IRS has received electronically from an employer the information that was sent to you on say a W-2, they may adjust your refund or tax liability accordingly before you do.

You still might have to file an amended return.

Bad Tax Idea: Taking an illegal tax position.

Good Tax Idea: Know what you can and can take legally.

What are some illegal tax positions? Here are some of the more common ones:

Thinking that you don't have to pay any taxes because they are unconstitutional.

Bad interpretations of Tax Court cases.

Claiming that only income earned from outside the United States is taxable.

Every few years some celebrity gets caught and made an example of non-payment of taxes. It is looking like Wesley Snipes, the actor from Blade, Passenger 57, White Men Can't Jump, New Jack City, etc. is turning out to be the IRS poster child of how not to have one's taxes completed. Willy Nelson, the country singer who was the former poster child finally settled his accounts as far as I know. As of the printing of this book, I don't know what Mr. Snipes is doing to settle with the IRS.

If you Google Wesley Snipes and taxes on the internet you can find all sorts of articles that go beyond the scope of this particular point I am trying to hammer home.

Avoid all types of tax scams that challenge the legality or constitutionality of the tax system. This is not to say that you shouldn't challenge any particular provision of the tax code or any specific action of the

IRS when you feel you have a legitimate case.

Just please avoid any of the arguments associated with the tax-protest movement that have already been defeated numerous times.

Any claim for religious entitlement, falsifying filing, etc. is also discouraged since the IRS has started fining people at least $500 for omitting sources of income or taking positions that are not legal.

Bad Tax Idea: Not differentiating between a Hobby or a Business.

Good Tax Idea: Learn the differences between a hobby and a business and how the IRS treats them.

There are differences in how we treat businesses and hobbies when it comes to taxes. On an individual return, business losses can offset other income, but hobby losses cannot. Therefore, it is important that you understand the difference between a hobby and a business.

How do you know if you are running a business?

For an activity to be considered a business, it must have a profit motive. You do not necessarily need to make a profit, but you need to show clearly that you are running a business and that the efforts and motivation are to further your business interests - and ultimately make a profit some day!

What does the IRS consider a hobby? A hobby is something done primarily for personal pleasure or recreation.

The general rule for profitability is that the IRS presumes an activity is engaged in for profit if the activity was profitable in three of the last five tax years, including the current year. As a taxpayer, you can accept this as gospel from the IRS. That being said, the three-years-of-profit test is not law, but a very good guideline that should be respected.

The one exception that I am aware of outside of the three year law is that for businesses dealing with horses (breeding, training, showing and/or racing), you have two of the last seven years to prove that it isn't a hobby. The presumption there is that it is harder to make money raising horses!

If you've been running your business for at least five years, you have a track record to determine yourself how things are going. If you have just started your business, you should consult with your tax preparer or financial planner.

You might see about postponement of the determination...There is a form, Form 5213, Election To Postpone Determination as To Whether the Presumption Applies That an Activity Is Engaged in for Profit, that can postpone the determination if you want to wait five years and see how your new business goes. Again, you need to research yourself if this is in your best interests or not. Generally, my take on this is that it isn't a good idea because:

1. You need to file Form 5213 separate from your tax return or else it will cause processing problems.
2. You pretty much have given yourself a red flag with the IRS by calling attention to yourself by sending in this form that   you think what you are doing may not be a business.
3. You extend the statute of limitations on whatever activity you are involved in. Filing Form 5213 extends the statute of limitations for assessing any income tax deficiencies attributable to the activity during any of the five preceding years. The period is extended to two years after the due date of the last tax return in the five year period. If the business does not go so well, you may find yourself finding it a little harder to get out from under the rock..

Another thing about the three-years-of-profit out of five years test - you could have the profit motive (I hope you do since losing money in a business really sucks-especially then to have it deemed a hobby by the IRS!) and have profits in less than three out of five years and still be considered a business. How does that work? You need to show the nine profit factors:

The Nine Profit Factors
The determination of whether an activity is engaged in for profit is ultimately based on the facts and circumstances of each person's business situation. The facts and circumstances must indicate that the taxpayer has a profit motive. The expectation of a profit may be remote or unreasonable, but it needs to be present. In some instances, it may be sufficient that there is a small chance of making a large profit. However, keep in mind that the taxpayer's statement that he or she is trying to make a profit must be backed up by facts. IRS regulations list nine profit factors that may be taken into account in determining whether an activity is engaged in for profit. No single factor is definitive on

its own and factors other than those listed may be considered. Not all factors apply in each case.

Descriptions of each of the nine profit factors follow.

1. Businesslike Manner. Importance is placed on whether the tax-payer carries on the activity in a businesslike manner. If the taxpayer carries on the activity in a businesslike manner, he or she is more likely to convince the IRS, or the tax court, that the activity is for profit.
Keeping good records, maintaining separate personal and business checking accounts, and having a written business plan are all indicative of a profit motive. So are marketing efforts that establish you are trying to get out there and sell your product or service!

Changing the methods of operating the activity to reduce costs or increase revenues can be evidence of a profit motive.

Under certain circumstances, ceasing operations altogether can be evidence of a profit motive.

2. Expertise. Importance is placed on whether the taxpayer, or the taxpayer's advisors, have the expertise needed to carry on the activity as a successful business. The more expertise a taxpayer has, the more likely the IRS will find a profit motive. Seeking knowledge through study or consultation with experts also indicates a profit motive.

If you as a business person study and consult with experts - you better take their advice otherwise will have difficulty showing a profit motive if he or she fails to follow the practices recommended. Make sure that your experts know what they are talking about!!

3. Time and Effort. Importance is placed on the amount of time and effort the taxpayer devotes to carrying on the activity. This is especially true if the activity does not have substantial recreational aspects. A taxpayer

who leaves an occupation to pursue the activity may be more likely to be viewed as having a profit motive. Also a taxpayer may show profit motive by employing others who invest time and effort in the activity.

4. Expectation of Appreciation. Importance is placed on whether the taxpayer can expect to make a future profit from the appreciation of the assets of the activity. The taxpayer's expected profit from the activity can include the potential increase in the value of assets used in the activity.

5. Success in Other Activities. Importance is placed on whether the taxpayer was successful in making a profit in other activities in the past. If the taxpayer was profitable in a similar activity, it may indicate he or she is engaged in the present activity for profit.

Prior experience, however, can be a double-edged sword. When a tax-payer has previous experience in a similar activity which was a hobby, the court is likely to rule that the current activity is a hobby as well.

6. History of Income and Losses.
Importance is placed on the history of the income and losses of the activity. A series of years where there was profit would indicate a profit motive.
On the other hand, ongoing losses undermine the claim of a profit motive. Although, they do not necessarily disprove a profit motive.
Losses beyond the control of the taxpayer do not indicate a lack of profit motive. Examples of losses beyond the control of the taxpayer include drought, disease, fire, theft, weather damage, involuntary conversion, and depressed market conditions.

Also, appropriate losses in the start-up phase of a business do not necessarily indicate a lack of profit motive. The amount of time necessary to reach profitability varies with the type of activity. Farming, inventing, and artistic endeavors are some examples of activities where diligent effort over a long period of time is often necessary before profits are made.

7. Occasional Profits. Importance is placed on whether the activity makes a profit in some years and the amount of the profits. The amount of profits in relation to the amount of losses incurred may provide useful information in determining the taxpayer's intent. Also, the amount of the taxpayer's investment and the value of the assets compared to the profits can be used to assess the profit motive.

An occasional small profit from an activity in which the taxpayer has made a large investment generally would not demonstrate a profit motive. However, an occasional substantial profit (compared to investment) generally would indicate an activity is engaged in for profit. Even an opportunity to earn a substantial latter profit in a speculative venture is usually sufficient to indicate the activity is engaged in for profit.

8. Dependency on Income. Importance is placed on whether the taxpayer depends on the income from the activity for his or her livelihood. The fact that the taxpayer does not have substantial income or capital from sources other than the activity may indicate the activity is engaged in for profit. On the other hand, income coming in from other sources may indicate the activity is not engaged in for profit. The IRS has been particularly skeptical when the losses from the activity generate large tax benefits. Again, that is something to keep in mind – keep things in the realm of reality, not the realm of impossibility. Figure that the IRS has heard it ALL before!

9. Element of Personal Pleasure. Importance is placed on whether the taxpayer is in the activity for personal pleasure or recreation. The mere fact that the taxpayer enjoys his or her activity does not mean it will be treated as a hobby. Nevertheless, elements of personal pleasure can have a detrimental impact on establishing a profit motive, and the

absence of pleasure can help establish a profit motive.

Bad Tax Idea: Confusing investment income - especially from rental property with earned income.

Good Tax Idea: With the huge surge in the last few years with "flipping houses" and the potential home sales market crash or softening it is important to learn the difference between business investment income and earned income.

BUSINESS INVESTMENT INCOME VS. EARNED INCOME

All payments received for the occupation or use of property is rent. However, there is a distinction between rent received as business investment income and rent as earned income.

1. Usually rent received for the use of real property and personal property leased with real property (for example, a washer or dryer or other appliances in a rental house) is business investment income unless services are provided with the property.

2. Any rent received in the ordinary course of a real estate dealer's business for the use of real property is business earned income. A real estate dealer is someone who is in the business of buying and selling real estate. Real estate professionals who are involved in "flipping" (i.e. buying real estate with the intention of selling it for a profit in a short time frame) are usually considered dealers. Also, builders and contractors who build houses and sell the finished houses to customers are also considered dealers. It is possible for a real estate dealer to have both business investment income and business earned income. Keep in mind that the IRS is going to be looking at this pretty closely for abuses due to the explosion (and slight busting) of real estate business in the last few years.

3. Rent received for the use of personal property is business earned income if the property owner is regularly engaged in the business of renting personal property. Business investment income and related expenses are reported and deducted on Schedule E.

Business earned income and related expenses are reported and deducted on Schedule C.

Net profit is subject to self-employment tax under the usual rules. Income from casual rental of personal property is reported on line 21, Form 1040.

If the taxpayer is not in the business of renting personal property but did have a profit motive, expenses associated with such rentals are deducted as a write-in on line 35, Form 1040, with the marginal notation "PPR." (That is for the current 2007 tax year returns as of the printing of this book).

If the taxpayer does not have a profit motive, the activity is considered a hobby and expenses, up to the amount of income reported, are deductible on Schedule A, subject to the 2%-of-AGI limit. The previous information is current as of 2007 and the gentle reader is cautioned to always check current tax law or with a tax professional before filing to stay current with form and law changes!

Good Tax Idea: Learning about Rental Income and Expenses and taking advantage of it.

Bad Tax Idea: Getting confused, greedy or downright illegal about Rental Income or Expenses when the law is pretty clear cut.

RENTAL INCOME

Business investment rental income is reported on Form 1040, Schedule E. For cash basis taxpayers, rental income is

reported in the year it is actually or constructively received. It is easy to recognize the payment made by a tenant at the beginning
of each month as rental income. However, other money payments are also considered rental income:

• Security deposits. When a property owner does not return a tenant's security deposit, it must be included in rental income.

• Lease cancellation payments. When a tenant pays a penalty for early release from a rental agreement, the payment must be included in rental income.

• Advance rent payments. Advance payment of rent is included in rental income the year received, regardless of the period covered by the payment. Advance rent includes:

– Payment for the last month of a lease period when paid at the time the lease is signed.

– A security deposit specified as covering final rent if not used for damages.
Remember if a tenant doesn't pay his or her rent in a timely manner, don't include uncollected rent in your rental income!!!!

Advance rent that is refunded is deducted as a rental expense.

• Insurance proceeds. Payments received for loss of rental income because of fire or other casualty are included in rental income in the year received.

• Direct tenant payments. When a tenant directly pays property expenses such as the mortgage, real estate taxes, insurance, or repairs, the payment must be included in rental income. Note: The property owner also deducts these amounts as rental expenses if applicable.

• Payments as part of property sale. Prepaid rents, received from a seller of rental property and attributable to periods after the purchase, are rental income to the buyer.

In addition to money payments, payments provided in the form of rendered services or exchanged property are rental income.

• The value of a tenant's services rendered to make repairs or improvements to a property in exchange for reduced rent or rent free use of the property is rental income.

– The property owner also deducts the value of repairs as an expense and depreciates any improvements.

– The value of improvements made by the tenant for his or her own use or convenience (not in place of rent) is not rental income.

• The value of property given to the property owner as payment of rent is included in rental income.

How about Security Deposits Held in Account? If a property owner is required by state law to put all security deposits for residential leases in a single interest-bearing account, a grantor trust is established. The interest and deposits belong to the tenants. The property owner may withhold a reasonable fee for administrative expenses and is responsible for filing Form 1041 if the interest earned is $600 or more. See the IRS instructions for Form 1041 if this applies.

The tenants are the grantors. Each tenant must report his or her share of the interest income and may deduct on Schedule A his or her share of the fee paid to the property owner. If the interest income is more than $10, it will be reported to the tenant on a Form 1099-INT by the bank that has the trust account. Each tenant's share of the fee is considered an investment expense and, as such, is subject to the 2%-of-AGI limit.

RENTAL EXPENSES
The owner of rental real estate deducts from gross rental income all expenditures necessary for the production of the rental income. The expenses are usually deducted in the year paid. Expenses are deducted on Schedule E, lines 5-20 .
• Auto and travel, line 6. Property owners deduct all ordinary and necessary auto and travel expenses related to the rental activity including trips to purchase supplies and repair materials, show the property to prospective tenants, collect rent, inspect the property, and maintain it.
The rules for business mileage apply: the taxpayer may deduct actual vehicle expenses or the standard mileage rate. If

the property is outside the taxpayer's tax home, the taxpayer may also deduct 50% of actual meal expenses or the standard meal allowance. Auto and travel expenses incurred as part of an improvement project are not deducted, but included in the depreciable basis.

• Insurance premiums, line 9. Prorate the premium paid for the number of months of coverage during the year if the coverage extends beyond the current tax year. Remember to deduct any premiums for the current year that were paid in an earlier year.

• Legal and other professional fees, line 10. Fees for tax services allocable to rental income and expenses, including preparation of Schedule E and related worksheets are deductible.

• Mortgage interest, line 12. Mortgage interest paid on rental property is deductible. Points (also called loan origination fees, maximum loan charges, or premium charges) paid on a mortgage for investment property are usually amortized and deducted over the course of the loan. If rental property is refinanced, only interest allocable to funds used for rental or other business or investment purposes is deductible. If the mortgage holder uses funds to purchase a new boat or pay for improvements to a personal home or vacation property, the interest allocable to those funds is not deductible.

• Repairs, line 14. A distinction between repairs and improvements is required. Repair expenses are deductible, while improvement costs must be depreciated. Repairs keep the property in good operating condition and do not materially add to the value of the property or substantially prolong its life. Improvements add to the value of the property, prolong its useful life, or adapt it to new uses.

• Taxes, line 16. Real estate and personal property taxes are deductible, but special assessments paid for items such as street paving, sidewalk improvements, and installation of sewer and water systems are not. Special assessments, taxes left unpaid by the seller, and taxes paid during the property's construction (after 1986) are added to the basis of the property. • Other, line 18. Enter expenses not covered under

other line categories. Wages paid for casual or contract labor, as well as payroll taxes are deducted on this line. The value of the property owner's labor or unpaid labor of friends and relatives is not deductible.
• Depreciation, line 20. Depreciation on the rental property and improvements is deductible.

Rental Expenses Without Rental Income

An owner of rental real estate may have expenses without income. These expenses are either capitalized and added to the basis of the property or deducted on Schedule E depending on whether the property is in service, that is when it is ready and available for rent.

The taxpayer who purchases rental real estate and spends a period of time remodeling or otherwise preparing the property, does not have the property in service.

Expenses incurred during this period may not be deducted. Instead they are capitalized and added to the basis of the property to be depreciated. The exceptions are mortgage interest and real estate taxes paid during this period. These expenses are deducted on the property owner's Schedule A: the mortgage interest is deducted on line 22 as investment interest and the real estate taxes on line 6.

Once the owner places the property in service, ordinary and necessary expenses, including depreciation, to manage, conserve, and maintain the rental property from the time it is made available for rent and the time it is rented may be deducted on Schedule E.

The owner continues to deduct the ordinary and necessary expenses, including depreciation, while the property is vacant between tenants as long as the property is available for rent. However, any loss of rental income is not deductible for the period the property is vacant.

Bad Tax Idea: Confusing Tax Refunds with Net Worth.

Are you one of those people who screams out "Hooray, I am getting a large tax refund?" If so, you may want to think what would you have been able to do with the money had you invested it yourself over the year.

You are giving the Federal and respetive state governments interest free loans of your money for the year. If you are the type of person who does this to create "forced savings" and that is the only way you can save money - okay, whatever works for you.

I just want you to realize that you might have been able to invest the money yourself or pay down credit cards/bills yourself and save yourself some interest payments or make some interest!

At the end of the year, it is how much money you are worth that is important and not how much of a refund you are getting back. If you are getting deeper into debt and getting a large refund, you aren't doing something right. You should be using that money to pay down your debt and start managing your resources.

You want your net worth to increase each year. Your net worth is calculated by taking the value of all your assets and subtracting out all of your liabilities.

So, if you have a home valued at say, $100,000 and you owe a mortgage of $80,000 and you have in savings $20,000 and credit card debt of $13,000 your net worth would be:

$100,000 – 80,000 + 20,000 – 13,000 = $27,000.

It should give you a sobering idea of how far away you are from your million dollar net worth!

That leads to the next idea..

Good Tax Idea: Start planning for where you want to be 3, 5, 10 and 25 years from now.

Start planning on where you want to be. Start with the short term goals and proceed to your long term goals. You won't get there unless you design the roadmap yourself. A few people I know have retired in their early fifties. They weren't millionaires - they just planned their live accordingly to live with minimum needs, only splurge on a few things and practice intelligent investing. Barring some life altering events, it isn't that hard if you stick with a plan, are patient and are trying to work.

Bad Tax Idea: Both Parents Claiming the kids if you are divorced.

The IRS and respective state taxing authorities cross check records and if both divorced parents try to claim the children, whoever filed second loses the race. Consequently, both parents may then have their tax returns reviewed to see if either of them can claim the children. Even if you are not on speaking terms with your ex-spouse, please be clear as to who is claiming the children on your tax returns.

Bad Tax Idea: Ignoring IRS or state taxing agencies letters.

If you get a letter of the IRS or a state taxing authority you generally have between 30-60 days to respond based on what the letter says.

Do not ignore the letter. If you ignore the letter, whatever claim they are making stands and you will not have a chance to object or question it.

Say for example you get a letter saying that you received savings account interest of $10000 instead of $100. You will probably have to mail back to the IRS your 1099-INT as well as the last savings account statement from December to show that you did not make that kind of interest.

If you ignore the letter, you will end up owing taxes on $9,900 worth of interest you did not receive.

That example is a little on the high side but you get the idea. Things like that sometimes happen if numbers are not scanned correctly, transposed or added accidentally as well.

I would suggest you send the letter back registered mail with a return receipt or tracking number or take it down to the local IRS or state agency office yourself if you have the time to prove your compliance that you responded in time.

Again, the rule of thumb is you should be saving your critical receipts and tax returns for at least three years from the date you filed the returns. Be prepared to save things longer if it involves things such as rental property, or any other long term asset.

Bad Tax Idea: Backing down from the IRS or state taxing agency if you think you are right and have evidence to support your claim.

If you think you are right and have evidence to support your claim, take whatever deduction or exemption you can as long as it is not something illegal. The IRS looks to see if your stance has a one in three chance of being supported - that isn't bad odds at all. If they deny your claim, you just pay what you owe. There is a chance that you will not be fined again if there was a one in three chance of the claim being supported.

Just don't take stances that are blatantly illegal such as the claim that you don't have to pay income tax or outlandish claims that you don't have the evidence to support with.

Bad Tax Idea: Not Understanding the Home Office or Business Deductions

Whenever you take the home office deduction, you have to remember to recapture what you deducted when you sell your home. The home office deduction affects the basis of your home.

Remember also that the home office deduction means that the particular area of your house, condominium or apartment that you use for your business must be used exclusively for your business.

The same goes for anything else that you are claiming you use 100% of the time at home for business.

If you are using a computer at home, it better not have any video games, internet games like World of Warcraft running, etc. if you are claiming it 100% for business. Also, it better make sense for your particular business that what you are claiming can be claimed. For example, if you do contract computer programming and have a computer that you use exclusively for work, there shouldn't be any problems using the machine.

If however you are a sanitation engineer (garbage collector), you will have to really document how you are using your computer 100% of the time for business, for billing, collections, offering some software where clients can look at colors, things like that in order to claim 100% use of your machine. Chances are for vocations like that you may have your deductions disallowed.

Now that we have determined if something is reasonable to be deducted, we see how much depreciation we can take for the item or the specific room in the house.

Good Tax Idea: Get to know the measurements of your entire house and the room or area that you are planning on using for your business for tax purposes.

It will simplify things for you later on at tax time.

Depreciation is generally calculated using tables that are available in most tax books, software packages or the IRS website (www.irs.gov). State depreciation can be found usually on the respective state sites.

Make sure that when you move onto your next year's taxes, if you are running software on your own or through the web, that you are picking up the running outstanding value of the house with the appropriate depreciation being deducted.

Good Tax Idea: Picking the correct business entity when going into one's own business.

One of the worst things a person (or group of people) can do is pick the wrong type of business entity when they are starting up a business. There have been horrible web offers and bad information telling people to incorporate to save money and take advantage of tax breaks so they will not only have a zero tax liability – they will get money back.

It is baloney.

In states where there is a state tax, a lot of them have an incorporation tax as well as other laws regarding employment taxes, social security taxes and a plethora of other compliance issues. In California for instance, if you incorporate, whether you make money or not, you are on the hook for a minimum tax of anywhere from $600 – 800 depending on what the tax law says the minimum payment is for that year.

That has been a nasty surprise to a lot of people who started up their business late in the year and find themselves on the hook for at least a minimum payment at their respective state level!

There are also a lot of required filings that you must comply with – whether you are making money yet or not – if you opt for incorporating.

My suggestion is to start small with a sole proprietorship and as you grow, you can either become a partnership, C Corporation or an S Corporation.

Are Corporations audited more than individuals? No more or no less if they are not fitting into whatever profiles that the IRS and the respective states have programmed into their software for kicking out tax returns for review (or even just line items for review).

Do you know the differences between the three types of business models?

Here is a quick review in terms of tax information:

Sole Proprietorship – One owner, who has unlimited personal liability for the obligations of the business. Say you start up John Doe's Hamburgers and somebody chokes and dies on your burger, you get sued and they can go after all your assets. Your taxes are filed on a Schedule C and your business isn't taxed, your profits or losses are passed through to you, the solr proprietor.

Generally, the only legal filings you have at the simplest level, depending on your type of business, is a DBA (Doing Business As) filing where you advertise in a newspaper for several weeks stating you will be using a certain name for doing business. After the publishing of the filing, you can take a clipping from the newspaper to your bank and open a checking account with the name of your DBA.

Two other items of note with a sole proprietorship are that – you manage your business and you contribute whatever capital is needed. If say, from our previous example, the hamburger business is good, and you want to raise money, you would go to a local bank and they would look at your assets, the business, etc and make the decision to loan YOU the money for the business or not.

The next type of business that is a step up in complexity from a Sole Proprietorship is a Partnership. Partnerships come in two flavors – Limited and General.

In terms of ownership- you can have an unlimited number of partners in both the limited and general partnerships with unlimited numbers of general and limited partners in the limited partnership.

For liability issues – in the general partnership, there is unlimited personal liability of the general partners for the obligations of the business.

For a limited partnership, there is unlimited personal liability of the general partners for

the obligations of the business and the
limited partners generally have no personal
liability.

For both limited and general partners, the
partnership is not taxed per se, the profits
and losses are passed through to the
general or general/limited partners. The
Federal form 1065 is usually used for
partnerships.

To file for a partnership you need a General
Partnership Agreement and whatever local
filings if your partnership holds real estate.

For a Limited Partnership you need a
Limited Partnership Certificate and a
Limited Partnership Agreement.

Who manages a partnership? In the
general partnership there is equal
management say between the partners
unless they have agreed otherwise. For the
limited partnership, the general partner
manages the business, subject to any

limitations of whatever was spelled out in the Limited Partnership Agreement.

Money is raised for the general partnership by contributions of money or service from the partners who receive an interest in profits and losses. In a limited partnership, the general and limited partners generally behave the same way.

Corporations generally are the most complex of the business entities and come in three flavors:

LLC – Limited Liability Corporation

C Corporations

S Corporations

In terms of ownership size, the C Corporations and the LLCs generally can have an unlimited number of shareholders. For the C Corp there is no limit on the different classes of stock that they offer. The S Corporation is generally limited to 100 members (I think that number is right

– I may be off so please double check yourself if you are planning on opening an LLC with over 100 members!) and is only allowed to issue one class of stock.

For all three types of corporations there is generally no personal liability of the shareholders for the obligations of the corporation.

Usually Form 1120 is used Federal Corporation taxes. Taxes for the LLC are not taxed (unless chosen to be taxed), as the profits and losses are passed through to the members.

S Corporations are generally not taxed as the profits and losses are passed through to the shareholders ("pass-through" taxation).

C Corporations are taxed on its earnings at the corporate level and the shareholders have a further tax on any dividends distributed (subject to some exclusions) (This is also known as "double taxation").

The legal documents you generally need for an LLC are – Articles of Organization and an Operating Agreement.

The C Corp needs Articles of Incorporation, Bylaws, Organizational Board Resolutions, Articles of Incorporation, Stock Certificates and a Stock Ledger.

The S Corp requires Articles of Incorporation, Bylaws, Organizational Board Resolutions, Articles of Incorporation, Stock Certificates, Stock Ledger and the IRS & State Corporation election.

An LLC is managed by the Operating Agreement which sets down how the business is to be managed and a manager can even be designated to run the business.

For the C and S Corporations, the Board of Directors has overall management responsibility and the officers of the corporation have responsibility for the day-to-day operations.

Money is raised for an LLC through contributions from the members of money or services and they receive interest in profits and losses.

For a C Corp, shareholders generally purchase stock in the corporation – either common or preferred.

S Corp shareholders typically can only purchase one class of stock.

Okay, so you can see the different levels of complexity involved and generally most of the hassles start to occur from my experience as a tax pro at the state level where people did not research the state requirements for filing correctly or anticipate the level of complexity that corporations are subjected to.

Again a good rule of thumb is to start small, with a sole prop if you are running a small business for yourself initially and then build up as you need more liability coverage or need to raise more money.

Please remember this if you don't do anything else:

It is a lot easier to get into a complex and different business entity then to get out of it!

Some other bits of trivia that I have seen from over the years. In places like California, some corporations may be treated as shells if you are sued and they may go after your personal assets.

I recommend that if you are starting a complex business that you consult with an attorney who has experience in the particular business you want to start and get their opinion as well from a legal point of view.

Also, as warned above – plan your exit strategy in advance. Do you want to run your business all by yourself forever? Do you plan on selling it later on if you are too old to run it by yourself? Keep things like that in mind!

Good Tax Idea: Always double check your results if you are using a software package or web tax software.

There is always a chance that the software has not been updated for the current tax year as tax laws are sometimes not approved till later on.

Witness the tax forms for 2007 not being approved till Congress approved them in December 2007 after they had already printed! A lot of tax provisions that were continued were not added to the tax forms and that resulted in not only the tax forms requiring all sorts of alphabetical codes to indicate certain credits, etc but that forced the state taxing agencies to start their updates later on.

So if the state taxing agencies don't finalize their tax rules till after Jan 1 and you already have the state software you need to remember to check for updates!

And as we discussed, people want their refunds N-O-W. They may inadvertently gyp themselves out of a tax credit or worse, file using an incorrect form.

Again, it pays to double check your work and be patient if you are a do-it-yourself web filer or software package person.

For the rest of us, have a good, trustworthy tax preparer review the return and he or she should double check and be current on the filings, the software and any updates.

Bad Tax Idea: Tax advance loans.

Please plan and try and budget your money so that you can have enough to cover emergencies and expenses.

When you file your taxes, you may be asked if you want a tax advance loan also known as an instant money loan or some sort of tax advance loan.

Generally, they are horrible investments because of the high interest rates that the lenders charge for them.

I understand that some people want their money N-O-W and will pay a premium for it and I will give it to them myself if they want it that way.

However, since you are reading this for ideas to SAVE money and possibly MAKE money it doesn't pay to get an advance on your tax return for possibly 25-30% fee for the privilege of getting it in one to three days versus two weeks (with direct deposit).

That is just my opinion and think of it this way:

You have a refund coming of $1000. The annualized interest is coming out to $50 for a tax loan advance. That is enough money for an inexpensive dinner for two, and two first run movie tickets. Wait the two weeks till you get your refund and then celebrate with the money you saved if you want to throw the extra fifty bucks away!

Or that can almost pay for a video game for one of the new video gaming systems!

Again, that is just my opinion ☺.

COMMENTS?

I can be reached through the internet through the website:

http://www.kimgreenblatt.com

Please check out some of the other books that I publish – a portion of sales from ALL my books goes to research for the cure of Rett Syndrome. Rett Syndrome is a disease that affects one out of every 15,000 girls at birth.

Boys born with the Rett gene die at birth.

For specific tax information, please consult your tax preparer. If you are interested in me doing your taxes, please drop me an email and we can discuss it. Thank you for your interest!

List of State Taxing Authorities or Agencies

As far as I know, this list is current. You can also find a copy of the list online at: http://www.kimgreenblatt.com/hsfcp/state tax.htm

Alabama Department of Revenue
    http://www.ador.state.al.us/

Alaska Department of Revenue
    http://www.revenue.state.ak.us/

Arizona Department of Revenue
    http://www.revenue.state.az.us/

Arkansas Department of Finance and
    Administration
    http://www.state.ar.us/dfa/

California Franchise Tax Board
    http://www.ftb.ca.gov/

California Board of Equalization
    http://www.boe.ca.gov/

Colorado Department of Revenue
http://www.revenue.state.co.us/

Connecticut Department of Revenue
Services
http://www.drs.state.ct.us/

Delaware Division of Revenue
http://www.state.de.us/revenue/

District of Columbia Office of the
Chief Financial Officer
http://cfo.dc.gov/main.asp

Florida Department of Revenue
http://www.state.fl.us/dor/

Georgia Department of Revenue
http://www.etax.dor.ga.gov/

Hawaii Department of Taxation
http://www.state.hi.us/tax/tax.html

Idaho State Tax Commission

http://www.state.id.us/tax/home.html

Illinois Department of Revenue
http://www.revenue.state.il.us/

Indiana Department of Revenue
http://www.ai.org/dor/index.html

Iowa Department of Revenue and Finance
http://www.state.ia.us/tax/

Kansas Department of Revenue
http://www.ksrevenue.org/

Kentucky Revenue Cabinet
http://revenue.state.ky.us/

Louisiana Department of Revenue and Taxation
http://www.rev.state.la.us/

Maine Revenue Services
http://www.state.me.us/revenue/

Maryland Comptroller of the Treasury
http://www.comp.state.md.us/

Massachusetts Department of Revenue
http://www.dor.state.ma.us/

Michigan Department of Treasury
http://www.michigan.gov/treasury/
Minnesota Department of Revenue
http://www.taxes.state.mn.us/

Mississippi State Tax Commission
http://www.mstc.state.ms.us/

Missouri Department of Revenue
http://dor.state.mo.us/

Montana Department of Revenue
http://www.state.mt.us/revenue/

Nebraska Department of Revenue
http://www.revenue.state.ne.us/

Nevada Department of Taxation
http://tax.state.nv.us/

New Hampshire Department of Revenue
Administration
http://www.state.nh.us/revenue/

New Jersey Division of Taxation
http://www.state.nj.us/treasury/taxation/

New Mexico Taxation and Revenue
Department
        http://www.state.nm.us/tax/

New York Department of Taxation and
Finance
        http://www.tax.state.ny.us/

North Carolina Department of Revenue
        http://www.dor.state.nc.us/

North Dakota State Tax Department
        http://www.state.nd.us/taxdpt/

Ohio Department of Taxation
        http://www.state.oh.us/tax/

Oklahoma Tax Commission
        http://www.oktax.state.ok.us/

Oregon Department of Revenue
        http://www.dor.state.or.us/

Pennsylvania Department of Revenue
http://www.revenue.state.pa.us/

Rhode Island Division of Taxation
http://www.tax.state.ri.us/

South Carolina Department of Revenue
http://www.sctax.org/

South Dakota Department of Revenue
http://www.state.sd.us/revenue/revenue.h
tml

Tennessee Department of Revenue
http://www.state.tn.us/revenue/

Texas Comptroller of Public Accounts
http://www.cpa.state.tx.us/

Utah State Tax Commission
http://tax.utah.gov/

Vermont Department of Taxes
http://www.state.vt.us/tax/

Virginia Department of Taxation
  http://www.tax.virginia.gov/

Washington Department of Revenue
  http://dor.wa.gov/

West Virginia State Tax Department
  http://www.state.wv.us/taxdiv/

Wisconsin Department of Revenue
  http://www.dor.state.wi.us/

Wyoming Department of Revenue
  http://revenue.state.wy.us/

INDEX

www.ingramcontent.com/pod-product-compliance
Lightning Source LLC
Chambersburg PA
CBHW031814190326
41518CB00006B/327